Pirate Plays

CW00349727

by Stan Cullimore

Contents

Characters

Narrator

The Captain – the pirate in charge. He's not very clever and he forgets things!

Floss – the ship's mate. She thinks she should be in charge. She likes telling other people what to do!

Billy – the cook. His two favourite things are eating … and then eating some more.

Sally – the cabin girl. She is easily the cleverest pirate on the ship.

Nobby – the parrot. He talks a lot and likes to get people in trouble!

Longman

Edinburgh Gate
Harlow, Essex

Play One: *Where's the Captain?*

Far, far away, there is a city beside the sea. Tied up in a quiet little part of the dock, there is a pirate ship. It is a small and scruffy ship that could do with a lick of paint. It is called The Sitting Duck. *This is the story of what happens next …*

Narrator   One lazy, sunny day on board *The Sitting Duck* two pirates were lying on deck enjoying the sunshine.

(Sally sits up and looks around.)

Sally   Do you know where the Captain is, Billy?

Billy   No, I don't! And you know what? I don't care.

Nobby   I know where the Captain is. *(Squawk)*

Narrator   Nobby the parrot was perched on the ship's wheel.

Sally   Where is he then?

Nobby   The Captain's gone to see a man. *(Squawk)* About a map.

Billy   I hope he remembers to buy some more biscuits – we've nearly run out.

(Sally lies down, yawns and closes her eyes.)

Sally   Ah! This is the life for me!

Nobby   Being a pirate is best. *(Squawk)*

Billy   Yeah! I love being a pirate. You can do whatever you want to do …

Nobby   That's true.

Billy   Sally?

Sally   Yes.

Billy   Do you think you could pass me that last packet of chocolate biscuits, please? Someone has eaten all the other ones.

(Billy flicks biscuit crumbs off his tummy and sighs.)

Nobby	I know who ate the biscuits. *(Squawk)* It was Billy!
Narrator	If there was one thing that Billy loved doing – it was eating.

(Sally sits and picks up the packet of biscuits that is lying beside her. She rolls it across to Billy.)

Billy	Thanks, Sally. Now, can you be quiet, please, Nobby?
Narrator	At that moment the cabin door flew open and Floss came on deck.
Floss	Right you two lazy lumps. Have you finished painting the ship yet?

(Sally stands up. She looks puzzled.)

Sally	What are you talking about?
Floss	Painting the ship. Have you finished it yet?
Narrator	Sally shook her head and frowned across at Billy.
Sally	Do you know what Floss is talking about, Billy?

(Billy puts down the packet of chocolate biscuits and tries to look innocent.)

Billy Well … er, sort of.

Floss What do you mean, 'sort of'? I told you this morning that you and Sally had to paint the ship today.

Nobby Billy and Sally! Paint the ship! Paint the ship today!

Billy Shut up, Nobby!

Floss So, have you done it?

Sally Hmm. No …

Floss Why not? What have you been doing all day?

Nobby Billy's been eating biscuits! *(Squawk)*

Narrator Before anyone could say anything else, footsteps rang out on the gang plank. The Captain came on deck.

Nobby It's the Captain. Now you're in for it!

Captain A very good day to you all, my merry band of pirates. How are you all this fine afternoon?

Nobby *(Squawk)* They're in trouble!

Captain Who's in trouble?

Floss Sally and Billy – that's who!

Captain What have they done wrong this time?

Sally Nothing!

4

Floss   That's just what they've done – nothing! I told them to paint the ship and they haven't done it.

Billy   It's all my fault. I forgot to tell Sally that we had to paint the ship.

Captain   Paint the ship? We haven't got time for that! Look what I've got!

(The Captain holds up his hand and waves it from side to side.)

Narrator   The Captain showed them a piece of yellow paper. It looked very old.

Floss   What's that?

Sally   It looks like some sort of map.

Nobby   A treasure map! *(Squawk)* And I know where you got it!

Captain   Be quiet, Nobby! You're right, Sally – it is a map. A treasure map. We're going to use it to go and find ourselves some buried treasure. Come on – let's go!

Narrator   A few minutes later, *The Sitting Duck* slipped away from the dock and set sail – in search of treasure.

Play Two: *Sally Sets Sail*

Far, far away, there is a deep, blue sea. Sailing across the waves there is a pirate ship. It is a small and scruffy ship that could do with a lick of paint. On board there are four pirates and their pet parrot Nobby. They have gone to look for treasure. This is the story of what happens next …

Narrator	It was a lovely, sunny day – perfect for sailing across the deep, blue sea. On board *The Sitting Duck* everyone was busy doing what they did best. *(The Captain walks from side to side across the deck with his hands behind his back.)* The Captain was busy being in charge.
Captain	Come on, Floss! Hurry up and get that sail up – this wind will get us there in no time.
	(Floss is standing next to the ship's wheel. She nods.)
Narrator	Floss was busy telling other people what to do.
Floss	Look lively there, Sally! You heard the Captain. We have to hurry and get that sail up.
	(Sally is pulling on a rope to lift the sail.)
Narrator	Sally was busy doing all the hard work.
Sally	Well if you ask me, I think we could get this sail up a lot faster if someone would help me!
	(Nobby is perched on the ship's wheel.)
Narrator	Nobby was busy trying to get people in trouble.
Nobby	That Billy is such a lazy boy! *(Squawk)* Why isn't he up here helping Sally with the sail?
	(The Captain turns to Floss.)
Captain	That's a very good question. Why isn't Billy up here helping Sally with the sail?

Narrator   Floss thought for a minute. Then she shook her head.

Floss   I don't know, Captain. Shall I find out?

Captain   Yes, please.

(Floss turns to Sally.)

Floss   Look lively there, Sally! You heard the Captain. Go and find Billy at once and ask him why he isn't up here helping you with the sail!

Nobby   Lazy Billy! *(Squawk)* Bad Billy! Lying in his bed and doing nothing all day.

Sally   I don't have to ask him. I know why Billy's not up here.

Nobby   It's because he's a great, big, lazy pirate! *(Squawk)*

Sally   No, it isn't.

Captain   Why is it, then?

Sally   Billy isn't up here on deck because he's busy in the galley – making dinner.

Floss   Oh, is he? Well I'll soon sort him out!

(Floss went over to the ship's bell and pulled on the rope.)

Narrator   Everyone covered their ears as the ship's bell rang out. DING, DONG! The Captain pulled a face.

Captain   I do wish you wouldn't keep on doing that, Floss! You know the bell hurts my ears when you ring it like that!

Floss   Sorry, Captain. I keep on forgetting.

Narrator   The sound of footsteps came from below decks. Then Billy came out of the cabin door and went up to the Captain.

Billy   Did you ring the bell for me, Captain?

(The Captain shakes his head and points at Floss.)

Captain   No. She did.

Narrator   Billy went over to stand in front of Floss.

Billy   What can I do for you, Floss?

(Floss points at the Captain.)

Floss   The Captain wants to talk to you!

Narrator	Billy went over to stand in front of the Captain.
Billy	What is it that you want to say to me, Captain?
Captain	That's a very good question. I'm afraid I can't remember at the moment. Can you remember what I was going to say, Floss?
	(The Captain turns to Floss. Billy sits down on deck.)
Billy	Well, when you DO remember what it is that you were going to say – let me know. All this walking about is making me tired!
Nobby	I know what it was. *(Squawk)* Billy's a great, big, lazy pirate!
	(The Captain shakes his head.)
Captain	No, that wasn't it.
Narrator	Billy scowled over at Nobby.
Billy	I am not a great, big, lazy pirate!
Nobby	Yes, you are. Sally said so!
	(Billy turns to look at Sally.)
Billy	Did you really say that, Sally?
Sally	No, I did not. Nobby is just trying to make trouble again – aren't you Nobby?
Narrator	Nobby bobbed his head up and down.
Nobby	Who's a pretty bird, then?
Billy	Not you! You're just a stupid, smelly old parrot with fleas! I should put you in the soup.
Captain	Oh, yes – that was it. I remember now. I wanted to ask you a question.
Floss	That's right – a question. Look lively there, Billy. The Captain wants to ask you a question.
Captain	What's for dinner today, Billy?

Floss	No, that wasn't it, Captain.
Narrator	The Captain blinked.
Captain	What was it, then?
Floss	You wanted to know why Billy was down in the galley making dinner when he should be up here helping Sally get the sail up.
Captain	That was it! Thank you, Floss.
Narrator	Floss smiled. Sally laughed.
Nobby	What's so funny?
Sally	There's no need for Billy to help me now.
Floss	Why not?
Sally	While you lot have been busy talking, I've been busy getting the sail up. See?
	(Sally points up at the sail.)
Narrator	The other pirates looked up. The sail was blowing in the wind. The ship was racing across the sea.
Captain	Well done, Sally! At this rate, we'll soon get our hands on that treasure

Play Three: *The Story of the Map*

Far, far away, there is a deep, blue sea. Sailing across the waves there is a pirate ship. It is a small and scruffy ship that could do with a lick of paint. On board there are four pirates and their pet parrot Nobby. They have gone to look for treasure. This is the story of what happens next …

Narrator   It was a lovely, sunny day. The wind was blowing and the sail was up. On board *The Sitting Duck* the four pirates and Nobby were on deck enjoying the sunshine.

(Sally looks up at the sail.)

Sally   Wow! It's really windy today, isn't it?

(Floss is standing next to the ship's wheel. She is playing Cat's Cradle with a piece of string. She nods.)

Floss   Yes, it is – nice and windy. Perfect weather for sailing.

Captain   It's a shame this old tub bucket of a ship of ours isn't in better shape.

Billy   Why is that, Captain?

Captain   Well, with this wind behind us we should be going a lot faster than we are!

Nobby   The Captain's right. *(Squawk)* We should be going a lot faster than we are!

(Floss looks up from her game. She is puzzled.)

Floss   But we are going fast, Captain. Very fast.

Captain   It's still not fast enough for my liking.

Sally   There's no hurry is there, Captain? That treasure map of yours looks very old.

Billy   What's the treasure map got to do with it, Sally?

Narrator   Nobby bobbed his head up and down.

(Nobby gets excited and starts flapping his wings.)

Sally Well, if the treasure map is old, then that means the treasure has been buried for a long time.

Nobby I knew that. *(Squawk)* Clever old Nobby.

Floss We all knew that, Nobby. It doesn't make you clever.

Billy What's your point, Sally?

Sally Well, if the treasure has been buried all this time – I'm sure it can wait a bit longer before we find it and dig it up.

Nobby I don't think so! *(Squawk)* I don't think so.

(Sally looks at Nobby and then at the Captain.)

Sally You know something about this treasure map, don't you, Nobby?

Nobby Yes. *(Squawk)* Clever old Nobby knows all about this treasure map.

Billy Then why don't you tell us what you know, Nobby?

Nobby Can't! *(Squawk)* It's a secret.

Narrator Floss finished her game and put the piece of string in her pocket. She scowled across at Nobby.

Floss The only thing that smelly old parrot knows is how to make trouble!

Sally I'm not so sure about that.

(Sally walks over to the Captain.)

Sally   Captain, do you know what Nobby is going on about?

Narrator The Captain bit his lip and looked down at his shoes.

Captain   Well … er, yes, I suppose I do really. It's something I meant to tell you – but I sort of forgot.

Billy   So what is Nobby going on about, Captain?

Captain   Er … it's about that treasure map I showed you.

Floss   What about it?

Sally   You haven't lost it, have you?

Captain   Oh no, it's nothing like that. In fact, it's quite the opposite.

Billy   What do you mean?

Nobby   Nobby knows. *(Squawk)* Clever old Nobby.

Narrator The Captain pulled the map out of his pocket and looked at it sadly.

13

Floss	You have to tell us what's going on, Captain. If you don't, that annoying little parrot will just keep telling us all how clever he is.
Captain	Well you see, it's like this …
Narrator	The Captain took a deep breath.
Captain	… It's not really my treasure map at all.
Nobby	I knew it. *(Squawk)* I knew it. Clever old Nobby.

(Nobby gets very excited. He bobs his head up and down and flaps his wings.)

Floss	That does it. I've had quite enough of listening to you – you annoying bird-brain.
Narrator	Before Nobby could move, Floss grabbed his beak with one hand. With the other hand she reached into her pocket and pulled out the piece of string. She tied it round Nobby's beak and smiled.
Floss	That will shut you up for a bit!
Nobby	*(Muffled squawk)*
Floss	Now what were you about to say, Captain? Something about the treasure map not being yours.
Captain	That's right. You see, I found it.
Billy	That's all right. You know the rule – finders keepers!
Sally	I'm not sure if that works with treasure maps, Billy.
Narrator	The Captain nodded sadly.
Captain	I think you're right there, Sally.
Floss	What do you mean?
Captain	Well, when I say I 'found' the map, what I really mean is that I saw it fall out of someone's pocket …
Nobby	*(Muffled squawk)*
Floss	That's not so bad!

Captain   … Then I put my foot on it so that he wouldn't see it lying on the floor.

Sally   That is quite bad.

Captain   It gets worse I'm afraid. When the other person asked me if I'd seen it, I said that I hadn't.

Billy   That is very bad.

Sally   You told a lie!

Floss   So who was this person – the one who lost the map?

(The Captain gulps and looks worried.)

Captain   Big, Bad Bob!

Floss   Oh, dear! That is very bad indeed.

Sally   Why? Who is this Big, Bad Bob?

Narrator   Floss looked out to sea and groaned.

Floss   I think you're about to find out. Look!

Narrator   Everyone looked. There was a black dot racing towards them over the waves.

Captain   That's his ship. He's following us. I think he wants his map back.

(Nobby gets rid of the string around his beak.)

Nobby   Yes! *(Squawk)* You're in trouble. Big trouble!

Play Four: *The Flying Pig*

Far, far away, there is a deep, blue sea. Sailing across the waves there is a pirate ship. It is a small and scruffy ship that could do with a lick of paint. On board there are four pirates and their pet parrot Nobby. They have gone to look for treasure. This is the story of what happens next …

Narrator   It was a lovely, sunny day – perfect for sailing. The wind was blowing and the sail was up. On board *The Sitting Duck* the four pirates and Nobby were on deck staring at a black dot that was racing towards them.

Floss   I think you should get your telescope out, Captain.

Captain   What for?

Floss   To see if that black dot racing towards us really is a ship.

(The Captain picks up his telescope and looks at the black dot.)

Sally   Well? Is it a ship, Captain?

(The Captain puts his telescope down and nods.)

Captain	Yes, I'm afraid to say it is.
Billy	Do you know which one it is?
Captain	Yes, I'm afraid I do. It's *The Flying Pig*.
Floss	Oh, dear. That ship belongs to Big, Bad Bob!
Captain	I know. And he's going to catch up with us very soon. His ship is much faster than ours.
Nobby	He's after you, Captain. *(Squawk)* He wants his treasure map back!
Floss	If you don't shut up, Nobby, I'll tie string round your beak – again.
Narrator	Nobby shut his beak and moved away from Floss.
Sally	So now what do we do?
Billy	There's only one thing we can do.
Sally	What's that, Billy?
	(Billy throws his arms up into the air and starts running around the deck.)
Billy	Panic! Aaaah!

Floss	Do be quiet, Billy, or else I'll tie my piece of string around *your* beak!
Narrator	Billy stopped running around and put his arms down. He looked confused.
Billy	But I haven't got a beak!
Sally	What Floss means is – can you just be quiet for a minute, Billy? We need to think about this.
Nobby	That's right. *(Squawk)* We need to think about this. *(Squawk)* Because some of us are in big trouble, and …
	(Nobby stops himself and looks over at Floss. Floss puts her hand into her pocket and brings out a piece of string.)
Floss	What did you say, Nobby?
Nobby	Nothing! *(Squawk)*
Billy	Yes, you did. You said that some of us were in big trouble.
Nobby	Er … it was a joke.
Captain	Hmm. What do you think we should do, Sally?
Narrator	Sally thought for a minute.
Floss	It's no good asking her, she's only the cabin girl. What does she know?

19

Sally	Well, I have got one idea that might work.
Billy	So have I.
	(Billy throws his arms up into the air and starts running around the deck again.)
Billy	Let's all panic! Aaaah!
Floss	I've still got my piece of string here you know, Billy.
	(Billy looks at the string that Floss is holding. He puts his arms down.)
Billy	Sorry.
Narrator	All eyes turned to the Captain.
Billy	What do you think we should do, Captain?
Captain	I still think we should listen to Sally. If she's got an idea – I want to hear what it is.
Floss	Why? It's bound to be a load of rubbish.
Sally	Can I borrow your telescope for a minute, please, Captain?
Captain	Of course you can, Sally.
Narrator	The Captain handed his telescope to Sally. She took it and looked out past the front of their ship. After a minute she put the telescope down and nodded.
Sally	I thought so!
Nobby	What? *(Squawk)* What is it?
Billy	Yes, go on, Sally. Tell us what you're thinking.
Sally	Well, what we should do is to give this treasure map back to Big, Bad Bob.
Floss	That might not be as easy as it sounds.
Sally	You're right! From what I've heard about Big, Bad Bob he sounds – well, quite scary.

Floss   He is! Believe me, I know. I once saw him pick someone up by their ears and …

Captain   Yes, yes, that's quite enough, thank you, Floss. We all know why he's called Big, Bad Bob.

Billy   I don't!

Nobby   I do. *(Squawk)* It's because he's very big, very bad and he's called Bob!

Sally   Exactly! Now, I don't think he's going to be in a very good mood when he catches up with us.

Floss   You can say that again!

Nobby   I don't think he's going to be in a very good mood when he catches up with us!

Sally   So I think we should leave the map on our ship – with a note saying 'Sorry' – then we should run away!

(Floss shakes her head and snorts.)

Floss   I told you her idea would be a load of rubbish. How can we run away when we're at sea?

Captain	I'm afraid that Floss has got a point there, Sally. You can't run over water.
Narrator	Sally laughed.
Nobby	What's so funny?
Sally	We don't have to run – we can row. See!
Narrator	Sally pointed at the small lifeboat tied to the side of the ship.
Sally	When I looked through the telescope I saw a little island up ahead. We can row there and wait for Big, Bad Bob to take his map and go away.
Captain	Great idea, Sally!
Narrator	A few minutes later Sally had written a note and left it on the table – along with the map. Then the pirates all climbed into the lifeboat and rowed away from *The Sitting Duck*.
Billy	I still think my idea was better!

Play Five: *Row, Row, Row Your Boat*

Far, far away, there is a deep, blue sea. Sailing across the waves there is a pirate ship. It is a small and scruffy ship that could do with a lick of paint. It is called The Sitting Duck. *Racing towards it there is another pirate ship. This one is called* The Flying Pig. *This is the story of what happens next …*

Narrator	It was a lovely, sunny day – perfect for sailing. The wind was blowing and on board *The Sitting Duck* the sail was up. But the ship was deserted. A small lifeboat slowly rowed away. On board there were four pirates and their pet parrot Nobby.
Sally	This rowing is hard work, isn't it, Billy?
Billy	Yes, it is.
Captain	Come on, you lot, no more talking. Put your backs into it and row! We need to go faster than this!
Floss	Look lively, you two. You heard the Captain – put your backs into it. We need to go faster than this or else Big, Bad Bob will catch us!
Captain	Do you have to talk about him, Floss? Just thinking about him makes me feel scared!
Nobby	I'm not surprised! *(Squawk)* He knows you stole his treasure map.
	(Sally puts down her oar.)
Sally	I'm sick and tired of rowing.
Billy	So am I – my arms are aching.
Captain	What are you doing, Sally? You can't stop rowing!
	(The Captain starts to jump up and down. He looks worried.)
Sally	I just have.

(Billy puts down his oar.)

Captain   Now Billy has stopped rowing too!

Billy   I know I have. My arms are aching too.

Floss   What do you think you're doing?

Narrator   The small lifeboat began to slow down.

Sally   We're going on strike – aren't we Billy?

(Billy nods. Now the Captain looks very worried.)

Captain   You can't do that.

Nobby   They just have!

Floss   But why?

Sally   We don't think it's fair.

Captain   What isn't fair?

Sally   Every time there's some hard work to be done, Billy and I always have to do it.

Nobby   That's true. *(Squawk)*

Narrator   The small lifeboat stopped moving forwards. It began to rock from side to side as the waves lapped against it.

(The Captain turns to Floss.)

Captain   They have got a point, haven't they? I mean, Sally and Billy always do the hard work.

Floss   Leave this to me, Captain. I know how to deal with these sort of people.

(Floss stands up.)

24

Floss	Now you listen to me, you nasty pair of smelly pirates …
Nobby	She called you a pair of smelly pirates! *(Squawk)*
Billy	I know she did – and it wasn't a very nice thing to do.
	(Billy folds his arms and looks out to sea.)
Sally	Calling us names won't help matters, Floss.
Captain	I think Sally is right there, Floss.
	(Billy turns to look at Floss.)
Billy	I mean – how would you like it if I called you a stupid old sausage face?

Narrator	Sally and the Captain both tried hard not to laugh. Somehow the name suited Floss.
Nobby	He called you a stupid old sausage face! *(Squawk)* And he's right!
Floss	Shut up, Nobby, or else you'll be doing the rowing from now on.
Billy	Nobby can't row – his wings won't hold an oar.
Captain	It's true, Floss. Parrots can't row – everyone knows that.
Nobby	It's not my fault!
Sally	When you lot have all quite finished – I've got an idea.
Floss	Not another one. What is it this time? It's bound to be a load of rubbish – as usual.

(Billy stands up and looks back at The Sitting Duck.*)*

Billy	Hey, look! *The Flying Pig* has caught up with our ship and Big, Bad Bob is going on board the *The Sitting Duck*.
Captain	Quick! What was that idea of yours, Sally?
Sally	I think we should all row. There are plenty of oars. We would get to that little island up ahead in no time.
Captain	Great idea, Sally. Right everyone, you heard her – pick up an oar and start rowing.
Narrator	The Captain pointed to the pile of oars in the bottom of the lifeboat.
Floss	What's the hurry, Captain? Once Big, Bad Bob finds his treasure map where we left it on *The Sitting Duck* he'll leave us alone.
Captain	Well … er, it's not going to be as easy as that, I'm afraid.
Billy	What do you mean?
Nobby	I know. *(Squawk)* The Captain's still got the treasure map.

(Floss groans.)

Sally	That's not true, is it, Captain?
Captain	Well … er, I'm afraid – that is to say …
Billy	He has still got the map. Look! It's sticking out of his pocket.
Floss	Now we really are in trouble. BIG trouble!
Sally	Captain! Why didn't you leave the map behind like we agreed?
	(Floss shakes her head and snorts.)
Floss	I know why – it's because he's a greedy old pirate who can't bear to give up on that stupid treasure.
Captain	I'm afraid that Floss is right. Sorry.
Narrator	Sally looked around at the other pirates.
Sally	In that case, there is only one thing we can do now.
Nobby	What's that?
Sally	Row as fast as we can and hope that we get to the island before Big, Bad Bob finds out that our Captain has kept the treasure map!
Narrator	Without another word the four pirates picked up the oars and began to row towards the little island as fast as they could.
	(Nobby sulks in a corner.)
Nobby	It's not my fault I can't row.

Play Six: *Treasure Island*

Far, far away, there is a deep, blue sea. Sailing across the waves there is a pirate ship. It is small and scruffy and could do with a lick of paint. It is called The Sitting Duck. *Beside it there is another pirate ship. This one is called* The Flying Pig. *They are both quite close to a little island. This is the story of what happens next ...*

Narrator	A small lifeboat glided in towards the little island. On board there were four pirates and their pet parrot Nobby. They reached the beach and got out of the lifeboat.
Billy	What do you think Big, Bad Bob will do when he finds out that we've still got his treasure map?
	(Sally looks out to sea at the two pirate ships floating side by side.)
Sally	One thing's for sure.
Nobby	What's that, then? *(Squawk)*
Sally	He will NOT be very happy.
Floss	You can say that again! Big, Bad Bob loves treasure. He'll be madder than a goat when he finds out that our Captain has still got the treasure map.
Captain	Can we all stop talking about Big, Bad Bob, please? It makes me feel nervous.
	(The Captain looks worried.)
Sally	We wouldn't have to talk about him if you had just left his treasure map back on *The Sitting Duck* ...
Billy	Like we agreed!
Floss	He would have found the map and left us alone.
Sally	Then we could have rowed back to the ship, sailed back to port and forgotten all about this stupid treasure map.
Narrator	The pirates all frowned at the Captain.

Nobby	Who's a stupid Captain, then? *(Squawk)*
Floss	I think we all know the answer to that one, Nobby.
Captain	Now that's not fair! I only took the map because I thought you lot would be pleased to find some buried treasure.
Floss	Why would we be pleased?
Captain	Well, we are pirates, after all. That's what pirates do – they dig up buried treasure. Hmmm?
	(The Captain looks around at the other pirates, hopefully.)
Sally	Not when it belongs to Big, Bad Bob they don't!
Captain	Come on, we're not scared of him – are we?
Nobby	Yes, we are. *(Squawk)* We're very scared of him.
Floss	I've seen what he does when he gets angry.
Billy	What does he do?
Floss	I saw him lift someone up by the ears once.
Billy	Then what did he do?

Floss	He spun them round for a bit and then he …
Captain	All right, Floss, all right. We all get your point. There are lots of stories about just how big and bad Bob really is. But that doesn't mean that we have to be scared of him.
	(Billy nods.)
Billy	I'm not scared of him.
Captain	There you are. See? Billy's not scared of old Bob – are you, Billy?
	(Billy shakes his head.)
Billy	No – I'm TERRIFIED!
Narrator	With that, Billy threw his hands into the air and began to run around the beach.
Billy	Everyone panic! Aaaah! PANIC! Run for the hills before Big, Bad Bob bites our legs off!
Captain	Calm down, Billy. He doesn't bite people's legs off.
	(The Captain looks across at Floss.)
Captain	Does he?
Floss	I've never heard of him doing it.
Sally	But there's a first time for everything.
Narrator	For one moment the Captain looked as if he was going to cry. Then he threw his hands up into the air and ran after Billy – shouting as he went.
Captain	Everyone panic! Aaaah! PANIC! Run for the hills before Big, Bad Bob bites our legs off!
	(Sally and Floss looked at one another. They both shook their heads.)
Sally	I think it's time to use a bit of common sense.
Floss	I agree.
Sally	The first thing we need is that treasure map.

Floss   Don't worry, I'll be able to get that for you.

(Floss walks over to the Captain and calmly puts her hand into his pocket. She brings out the treasure map and takes it to Sally.)

Nobby   Now what do we do?

Narrator   Sally looked at the map carefully. She frowned. She turned the map over and looked at the other side. She smiled.

Floss   What's so funny?

Narrator   By way of an answer Sally held up the piece of faded yellow paper. The only thing on it was a list of words written on one side.

Sally   It isn't a treasure map at all – it's a shopping list!

Captain   What? A shopping list!

(The Captain puts his hands down, goes over to Sally and snatches the piece of paper out of her hands.)

Sally	All this fuss over a silly shopping list!
Captain	No, you must be wrong. Why would Big, Bad Bob chase after us just for a shopping list?
Nobby	Perhaps he wasn't chasing us. *(Squawk)* Perhaps he just wanted to say hello.
Floss	I think Nobby might be right. Look!
Narrator	Floss pointed out to sea. The others looked up in time to see *The Flying Pig* turn around and sail away.
Floss	How could you be so stupid, Captain? Fancy thinking a shopping list was a treasure map.
	(Billy cries out.)
Billy	Ouch!
Sally	Now what is it?
Billy	I've just stubbed my toe on something.
Floss	What?
	(Billy looks down and gasps.)
Billy	You're not going to believe this – but I think it's a buried treasure chest!
Narrator	You know what? It *was* a treasure chest. Soon the pirates were surrounded by a huge heap of gold and jewels.
Captain	Which just goes to show that sometimes being stupid is the cleverest thing of all!
Nobby	Rubbish! *(Squawk)* It was luck!